Your story matters!

JOEY'S STORY
A Long Way Home

Written by:
RODRICK JOHNSON

Ilustrated by:
MAURO PÉREZ

©2025 Rodrick Johnson
ISBN: 979-8-218-62218-3
All rights reserved. No part of this publication may be reproduced, distributed, or transmitted in any form or by any means, including photocopying, recording, or other electronic or mechanical methods without the prior written permission of the author at rjohnson@energizededucator.com

Blessed Publications
www.blessedpublications.org

I don't live with them all at the same time. I travel around and live with a different mommy as often as every week.

I am really good at packing my stuff in big trash bags in the blink of an eye because I move so much.

Before I move to a new mommy's house, I make sure I pack my favorite blue shirt. There's nothing special about it.

It's just my favorite. I always pack this shirt while singing "The Bare Necessities" song from *The Jungle Book*.

I have had so many mommies that I can't even count them all on my hands. Some of them were good like a Sunday meal and some of them were bad like a hot plate of vegetables.

I don't like vegetables much and I did not like those kinds of mommies.

I have a social worker that is my own special friend.
She dresses really nice and speaks with a serious voice.

She wears big glasses so that she can see the road when she is driving. She is so nice to me. When she talks, she smiles as bright as the sun.

My social worker always shows up when it is time for me to meet a new mommy. "Joey, I am taking you to a new house because the mean mommy was not good for you. She didn't treat you right."

So she moves me away to try another mommy. Sometimes, it feels like I am trying on clothes.

I try not to think about the mean mommies too much because it makes me sad.

Just imagine. Someone who's supposed to love you treats you bad just because they are not your real mommy.
It doesn't feel good at all.

The mean mommies' voices were like the sound of breaking glass, loud and scary. When a glass breaks, you know the pieces can't be put together again and you're in trouble.
When the mean mommies yelled, screamed and sometimes hit, I felt like that broken glass.
Like I could never be put back together again.

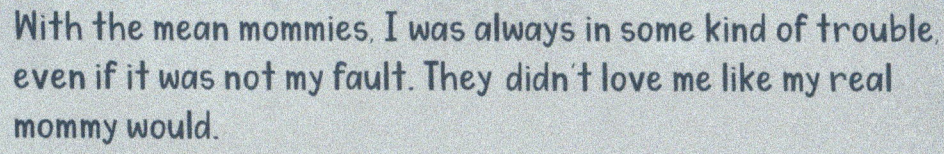

With the mean mommies, I was always in some kind of trouble, even if it was not my fault. They didn't love me like my real mommy would.

Sometimes I would sit and think:

> When am I going to meet my real mommy? I know one day I will move into her house and then I won't have to move anymore.

> Yes, I will hug her and never let her go because she will be all mine!
>
> She will also know that I was looking for her and she will say, "I love you."

My new mommy makes me feel safe and welcome.
She is a loving lady who lives in a big house.
She takes me to church where I sing on the choir.
They really like me at church and they give me a
lot of love there, especially when I sing.

Today, another child moved out and my new mommy gave me my own room. "Joey, you will stay with me until you meet your real mom. And guess what? You are going to meet her very soon."

I am so excited to meet her. I already know all the things that I want to say to her. Things like, "I love you" and "I am so glad that I was able to finally meet you!"

My sister is two years older than me so she will be able to teach me so much about our family. I imagine her as my older twin because we have the same mom.

My new mommy also taught me to keep smiling even if I feel hurt and never let the bad things that happen change who I am. She said, "Sometimes bad things happen but you must smile because there is always something to smile about. Even when you cannot see it right away."

That night I had a dream. I dreamed about what happened at the mean mommy's house. It was so sad. I remembered her screaming and yelling at me. I also remembered crying because she made me feel unloved.

I felt scared because of how the mean mommies treated me. They treated me like an old toy that they forgot to throw away. I was not special and I am glad that I do not have to deal with that kind of mommy anymore.

When I woke up, I reminded myself that as long as I have life and a smile everything will be okay. There is always a bright side somewhere.

The next day, my new mommy gave me good news! "Your real mommy wants to meet you Joey. And she wants you to meet the rest of your family."

I immediately imagined a big house where my real mommy and sister would teach me all kinds of things.
I imagined what my room would look like, what it would smell like and what food I would eat.
I really hope I have a good family.
I plan to walk in with a smile when I meet them.

When we drove to my real mommy's house, I could not keep from smiling! I knew that the love I wanted was there.

When we got there my whole family was sitting on the couch. My mom gave me the biggest hug. And I got to meet my own family! I could not believe that all these people were my family.

I thought I had a little family. But I met my real mommy, my sister and many others whose names I cannot remember because they got lost in my happiness!

Years later I was able to move in with my real mommy. I did not have to pack my things or move to another family ever again.
I still kept in contact with my last new mommy since they both took turns raising me.

When I moved in with my real mommy, I met my grandmother. She is so sweet. She is really short with a gentle voice that sounds like music.
And she always tells me how to be kind. I had so many people to help me be special. My mom, my foster mom and my grandma took turns raising me and I never had to pack my things again!

About the Author

Rodrick C. Johnson is a dedicated literacy coach, CEO, and founder of Energized Educator. With over eight years of experience, he has committed his career to reshaping educational spaces, empowering educators, and uplifting urban youth—particularly Black boys—through culturally responsive behavior support and restorative practices.

Inspired by his own journey through foster care, Rodrick wrote Joey's Story – A Long Way Home to provide hope to children facing similar challenges. His vision is to create a world where children are seen for their potential, celebrated for their unique perspectives, and supported through approaches that foster respect, responsibility, and readiness to learn.

Driven by the belief that every educator has the power to transform lives, Rodrick continues to spark positive change in school communities, ensuring that every child feels valued and empowered to succeed.

www.ingramcontent.com/pod-product-compliance
Lightning Source LLC
Chambersburg PA
CBHW042039160525
26716CB00007BA/58